Financial Management for Beginners

You Need a Budget to Manage Your Money. Personal Planning, Money Mindset and Discipline for Financial Independence

DAVID STOKES

ISBN: 978-1986146081

Text Copyright © David Stokes

All rights reserved. No part of this guide may be reproduced in any form without permission in writing from the publisher except in the case of brief quotations embodied in critical articles or reviews.

Legal & Disclaimer

The information contained in this book and its contents is not designed to replace or take the place of any form of medical or professional advice; and is not meant to replace the need for independent medical, financial, legal or other professional advice or services, as may be required. The content and information in this book have been provided for educational and entertainment purposes only.

The content and information contained in this book have been compiled from sources deemed reliable, and it is accurate to the best of the Author's knowledge, information, and belief. However, the Author cannot guarantee its accuracy and validity and cannot be held liable for any errors and/or omissions. Further, changes are periodically made to this book as and when needed. Where appropriate and/or necessary, you must consult a professional (including but not limited to your doctor, attorney, financial advisor or such other professional advisor) before using any of the suggested remedies, techniques, or information in this book.

Upon using the contents and information contained in this book, you agree to hold harmless the Author from and against any damages, costs, and expenses, including any legal fees potentially resulting from the application of any of the information provided by this book. This disclaimer applies to any loss, damages or injury caused by the use and application, whether directly or indirectly, of any advice or information presented, whether for breach of contract, tort, negligence, personal injury, criminal intent, or under any other cause of action. You agree to accept all risks of using the information presented in this book.

You agree that by continuing to read this book, where appropriate and/or necessary, you shall consult a professional (including but not limited to your doctor, attorney, or financial advisor or such other advisor as needed) before using any of the suggested remedies, techniques, or information in this book. The content contained within this book may not be reproduced, duplicated or transmitted without direct written permission from the author or the publisher.

Under no circumstances will any blame or legal responsibility be held against the publisher, or author, for any damages, reparation, or monetary loss due to the information contained within this book. Either directly or indirectly. You are responsible for your own choices, actions, and results.

DEDICATION

To my friends and family,
for giving me strength and support when I needed them the most.

To Donut,
the only cat that slept on my lap forbidding me to leave my writing workplace.

TABLE OF CONTENTS

Introduction 7
   Budgeting's negative reputation 7
   The true value of budgeting 7

Chapter 1: Budgeting Basics 10
   Create Some Goals 10
   Pay Close Attention To Your Net Income 11
   When You Create Your Plan 12
   Now it is time to personalize your budget. 13
   Making Your Budget. 13
   Check Your Spending Habits On A Monthly Basis 14

Chapter 2: Living Paycheck to Paycheck 16
   The Importance of Curbing Spending 16
   The Importance of Saving for the Future 17
   How Budgeting Helps You Meet Your Goals 18
   Methods of Budgeting 19

Chapter 3: Common Motivation for Budgeting 20
   Discovering Your Motivational Sources 22
   Make self-talk a habit 23

Chapter 4: How to Get Over Compulsive Spending Habits 24
   What is Compulsive Spending? 24
   Is Compulsive Buying a Mental Health Issue? 25
   How to Overcome Compulsive Buying 26

Chapter 5: Tackling Credit Card Debt 28
    The Most Important Rule 28

    Another Important Rule 29

    Your Credit Card Debt 29

    Snowball Method 29

    Avalanche Method 30

    Your Credit Score Is Important. 30

    Things You Should Know About Credit Cards 31

Chapter 6: Creating Your Budgeting system 34
    Step 1: Identify your financial priorities 34

        Identifying future financial needs 34

        Adding your passion in the list 35

    Step 2: Set the right amount of money for your needs and wants. 35

        Employing a budgeting rule 36

        80-10-10 Rule 36

        60-10-30 Rule 37

        50% Rule 37

    Step 3: Adjust your lifestyle and goals according to your income level 37

        Increase your income 38

    Step 4: Allocate your money as soon as you receive it 38

    Step 5: Track your money 39

Conclusion 42

INTRODUCTION

Common people only budget their money when they are short of funds. Financially successful people do it all the time.

Budgeting includes all the spending techniques that we apply to ensure that we spend less money than we receive. For most people, budgeting means making their current cash balance fit for all their needs and their wants until the next payday. Wiser people use budgeting as a way to prepare for the future and to reach their saving goals.

Budgeting's negative reputation

Because people tend to do budgeting only when they are low on cash, it creates a negative feeling in them. They feel bad when they follow a budget because it feels like that they are depriving themselves of the good things and experiences. They feel that they deserve to spend their own money any way they want. They want to gain good feelings from the money they worked hard for, and budgeting prevents them from doing that.

It is challenging to ask the people around you to follow a budget. The more you force people to limit their rewards, the more they want to spend. If you want your entire household to follow a budget, you need to 'package' it in a different way. Most professional financial planners, for instance, prefer to call it 'proper allocation of funds' to make their clients accept the idea of budgeting.

The true value of budgeting

When we follow a budgeting plan, we are not depriving ourselves. Rather, we are forgoing immediate gratification in exchange for greater rewards in the future. If you want to be successful in the long run, you need to practice letting go of instant gratification.

We practice this principle consistently in all areas of life. Most people already have the budgeting skills they need. Most of us know how to avoid unnecessary expenses. If you commute to work, for example, you may have selected a route that gets you to work with the least expenses. If we do not follow a budget, we would just take the most convenient means of transportation without thinking of the cost. Because we care about being efficient with our money, however, we usually avoid expensive forms of transportation.

You are already practicing budgeting in most areas of your life. For most people, their budgeting progress is ruined by just a few financial activities. One of the most common areas where people lack discipline is in eating out. This is a big challenge for most millennials. Other people fail to budget well because of expensive tastes in clothing.

A person may be disciplined in the way he spends his money on food, utilities, and groceries but when it comes to spending on things that make him happy, he loses control. If you want to reach your financial goals, you need to find out which financial activities hurt your budget.

By knowing about your spending weaknesses, you will be able to find strategies that will allow you to improve your budgeting performance in the future. You should practice budgeting every day. You should make budgeting a habit so that you will still practice it even when you are more financially stable. You should never stop budgeting. If you dislike smoking but still want to enjoy the natural miracle of cannabis, then this cannabis dessert cookbook is for you. This dessert cookbook will show you how to make delicious edibles with marijuana. Eating marijuana gives you a more powerful and longer high, spares your lungs, and allows you to enjoy in private. This makes it perfect for people who just want to add cannabis into food for enjoyment or patients who need steady relief from pain. This cookbook is specially designed for health-conscious beginner bakers who want to know how cannabis can be incorporated into baked goods. Making yummy cannabis desserts doesn't have to be a chore. With this cookbook's easy-to-follow instructions, it is simple.

Now you can make your edibles in the comfort of your home. If you enjoy sweet desserts, then you will love this cookbook. Do yourself a favor and make every dessert enjoyable and delicious by following the steps in the recipes that follow. This dessert cookbook will arm you with everything you need to decide for yourself if the edible cannabis is right for you. Just follow the simple methods to make some of the most satisfying cakes, cookies, brownies, cupcakes, and ice creams, and much, much more. All the recipes are amazingly tasty and delicious. This cannabis dessert cookbook is your go-to companion for daily enjoyment. If you want to try some absolutely delicious cannabis dessert recipes, then leaf over and start reading now!

CHAPTER 1: BUDGETING BASICS

It can be said that the hardest part about living on a budget is sticking to it. We always have the best of intentions when we create a personal or household budget but is "actually following the budget" that is the most difficult part of the whole situation. However, I would argue that forming the habit is the difficult part. After that habit is formed, it can be fairly easy to stick to it.

We don't all know what "living on a budget" entails. When you hear that phrase, what do you instantly think of?

"Having no fun."

"Saving all of your money."

Is that about right?

Create Some Goals

We are all in different parts of our lives. Because of this, we all have different financial obligations. Not only that, but we also want different things out of our futures.

Some of us want to be able to retire and travel. Some just want to be able to live in a tiny house. Other people want to be able to have vacations homes that they can visit when they feel the urge to move around. Some of us need to save for our families. Others just want some play money and money to live comfortably in the future.

Ask yourself what you want out of your life. What kinds of short term and long term goals do you have and how do you need to financially ready yourself for those goals? Keep in mind that short terms goals should take no longer than a year to complete while an example of a long-term goal would be, "Save for retirement" or "Put away money for my child's education."

Do you need to save a lot of money for a new house? To be ready for children? Or perhaps so you can start your own business. How long will it take for you to save up the necessary funds to make these goals attainable?

Remember that these goals aren't set in stone. Things happen in our lives that make us rethink what we want out of our future. You can change the items on this list as you grow older and experience more things.

Pay Close Attention To Your Net Income

One of the biggest pitfalls when it comes to planning out and living on a budget is creating and following a plan that is within your income. In a time where material possessions have become something of a status symbol, we have learned to live outside our means. This is one of the main reasons why a lot of people are in credit card debt and can't stick to a budget or save money.

The first step that you identify how much money you have coming in. Knowing your income is important. Some of you may have to estimate how much you have coming in every month because you own your own business, run a freelance or by-contract business, or because your income fluctuates.

If this is you, make sure that you underestimate how much income you bring in each month. I only suggest this because it is easy to overestimate and that will cause your budget to be unreasonable and unattainable.

Also remember to take into account your employer deductions for taxes, retirement plan, insurance, Social Security, and maybe spending account allocations.

When You Create Your Plan

When you create your budget plan - and you've found your average monthly income – divide your income into two big categories: fixed spending and variable expenses.

The expenses that would fit under fixed spending would include your utilities and bills that don't change much each month. This would include your mortgage, car payments, credit card payments, regular utilities, etc.

The items that would fit under variable expenses include expenses that change every month: entertainment, food (though this can fit in either depending on your habits), gas and travel expenses, etc.

I suggest that you record these expenses for a couple months to see what your trends and habits fall. If you are anxious to get a budget plan ready, I suggest that you look into your bank records. Online banking has made things incredibly easy these days. Some online banking accounts even break down your spending for you depending on where you shop.

My online bank account does that exact thing; they organize my spending habits by categories. This makes it much easier to keep track of where my money goes.

At the minimum, I would manually break up your spending into three different categories:

- Needs and necessities
- Savings
- Desires

Needs include the fixed and variable costs that are necessary to living a healthy life. The savings section would include both emergency funds and retirement. The desires section would cover everything else.

Now it is time to personalize your budget.

Okay, so you've analyzed your spending habits. Now it's time to personalize a budget. A great thing that is simultaneously obnoxious is the fact that every budget should be personalized. This means that you don't have to be pigeonholed into keeping a budget that doesn't fit your needs (Yay!). However, this also means that you have to work harder to come up with the perfect budget that does (Ooh...).

Okay, now that you've figured out what your fixed spending number is, set that aside every month so that you will always have that money available for important expenses. What you have left should be divided up into variable items. This number is also a variable in and of itself. If you allow a certain amount of things like clothes, but you know that you need to save for a TV, you can skim a little from your clothes fund and add that to your TV fund.

Making Your Budget.

Creating your actual budget can be done in as little as four steps after you've done all of that prep work.

1. Keep a record of your spending and analyze your results. Record your spending and have your significant another record theirs as well. I suggest keeping a small notebook and pen with you at all times for one month. In addition to that, keep a spreadsheet on your computer. Transcribe your.

2. Plan for your next month's spending. If you live with a significant other, make sure that you plan together and that you take all of your expenses into consideration, even if you both have separate bank accounts. You don't have to keep track of each other's "desired" sections. However, it is important to come up with a spending cap. When you want to buy something of a certain amount – which will differ with each couple – you may want to defer with each other. Some of you may not need to do this. Others feel that it is a

courtesy to one another. While others yet feel that it is necessary because you have joint accounts. My husband and I keep our own records for little spending. However, if something costs $100 or more, we mention it to each other. If something costs $500 or more, we discuss it as a team so that we can come up with rational and smart choices.

3. Look for ways that you can spend less. While spending a little bit for a long time can add up, so can saving a lot of money. Saving just a little bit over a long period can add up to some incredible savings. To do this, consider some of these options:

    1) Shop at a cheaper grocery store
    2) Buy generic brands
    3) Cook at home instead of eating out
    4) Entertain at your house instead of going out to a club or movie
    5) Utilize coupons during sales

4. You can also find ways to boost your income. If you have a hobby or talent, you may be able to use it to earn some extra money. Teaching your hobby to others can prove to be profitable. You can also sell your wares on an online shop, or at local markets. One great bonus is that you may be able to turn this side job into a full-time job if you ever lose your main source of income. Handy, huh?

Check Your Spending Habits On A Monthly Basis

Are you sticking to your budget? If not, where are you going astray and how can you fix that? Take a look at your spending every month and compare it to your budget worksheet to see how things are going. If you find that you're often going over-budget in some areas out of necessity, you should consider cutting elsewhere to keep things under control.

CHAPTER 2: LIVING PAYCHECK TO PAYCHECK

Are you tired of the constant feeling that you don't have any money? Living paycheck to paycheck is a real problem for many people. While some of the people in this rut are low earning families, many are not. Those in the middle class can also become entrenched in this cycle.

There is an old saying that you will spend what you earn. Generally, it is expected that you are living within your means and meeting all of your financial obligations. At the same time, you don't have any money left over. As you earn more money, you take on additional expenses or luxuries that eat up the additional income. This is how many families fall into the paycheck to paycheck cycle.

Breaking this cycle is possible. You have to have some willpower. You have to force yourself to deal with delayed gratification. Here are some tips for breaking the cycle.

The Importance of Curbing Spending

Most people who have trouble making ends meet or running out of money before the next paycheck hits spend quite a bit on unnecessary expenses. When you cut back on some of the luxuries of life, you will find that you can save vast amounts of money. Even if it is something as simple as choosing an off brand at the grocery store, all of those pennies and dollars add up quickly. Here are a few ways you can curb your spending.

1. Limit fast food trips to two per month
2. Buy off brands at the grocery store
3. Shop thrift stores for clothing before going to department stores

4. Limit entertainment such as movies and concerts to one per month
5. Cut out or cut down your cable or satellite bill
6. Cut back on cell phone usage and bills
7. Never use payday loans—they cost more than they're worth
8. Cut back on driving to the bare minimum to save on gas
9. Turn up the thermostat in the summer and down in the winter—dress for the weather instead of compensating with high energy bills
10. Cut out or cut back on vices such as soda and cigarettes
11. Make your desserts instead of buying prepackaged cookies and cakes

These are just some of the ways you can trim the fat from your spending. Carefully consider where you spend money that you don't need to spend. Anything you can cut back would be beneficial. At the same time, don't deny yourself every pleasure. You have to feel like you are benefiting from your frugal lifestyle and all of your hard work. Denying yourself every luxury all the time will cause you to give up on budgeting.

The Importance of Saving for the Future

One of the biggest problems with living paycheck to paycheck is that you don't save back any money for the future. Whether you are looking five years ahead or thirty, it is important to save at least a small amount from each paycheck toward your long-term goals.

Of course, the big savings goal many people think about is their retirement. If you are younger than 40, this event may seem so far in the future that it is hardly worth worrying about. However, this is the attitude that is leaving many middle-aged adults struggling to figure out what they are going to do when they have to retire. Saving money for your retirement needs to start at a younger age. If you start early, you can save a large amount of money without hurting your average income and spending.

Many other things are closer to the present that you might want to save up for. If you are close to any of these events, or you just want to be prepared for them in the future, you should start saving now. Here are just a few.

- A wedding for yourself or your child
- Preparing for a baby
- College tuition for a child
- A car that you don't have to make payments on
- A down payment on a house that will save you on housing costs
- A nest egg for maintenance or replacement of major appliances as they age
- A family vacation that your children will remember for a lifetime

Saving money isn't just about surviving. It's about living. Without saving back money for the little things, and the big things, that come along in life, you will fail to truly enjoy them when they arrive because you will be struggling to pay for them. Planning not only keeps you prepared for emergencies but also decreases stress and increases overall happiness.

How Budgeting Helps You Meet Your Goals

Budgeting is an important step in helping you meet your goals. Budgeting isn't just about being careful with your money. You can use budgeting tools to help you plan your income and spending so that you can intentionally set aside savings. You can use expense tracking to help you trim the fat from your budget and see where you can make changes to improve your overall quality of life, now and in the future. Your long-term financial goals, as well as your short-term way of life, can only be realized through effective budgeting.

Methods of Budgeting

There are three primary ways to budget. You can budget by a week or pay period, month, or by expense. Budgeting by expense is the easiest way to budget. It is done by using the envelope method, which will be explained shortly. Budgeting by a week or pay period can help you stop the paycheck to paycheck cycle, but works with that mentality while you work to improve your financial habits. Monthly budgeting is helpful because you can see everything you spend monthly at one time. This is important because many bills are only paid once per month.

You may choose to use a combination of methods. Sometimes it can be helpful to have even the most basic monthly budget to use in combination with a weekly budget. It can also help to use the envelope method, especially if you have difficulty setting aside money for larger expenses.

CHAPTER 3: COMMON MOTIVATION FOR BUDGETING

Budgeting can be challenging if you have not developed it into a habit. You need to make hard choices every day to implement your plan properly. You will be declining offers from friends to eat out or to buy more than one bottle of beer after work. The hardest challenge of all is to resist old habits that may be causing our financial problems.

In the beginning, you need to find ways to motivate yourself into budgeting. You need to have an excellent reason to save money. Most parents work hard and sacrifice their immediate gratifications for their children. Some people save up to fund continuing education. You should think of your reason for becoming efficient with your money.

You need to examine your situation and ask yourself why you need to start budgeting. Here are some reasons that may motivate you to start this habit.

- You will be able to save for great experiences

By budgeting every day, your family will be able to save for things that you normally would not be able to afford. If you know how to follow a budget plan, you will be able to save money that you can use for giving great experiences to your kids.

- You will be prepared for all expenses, expected or not

Budgeting allows you to save a part of your money for the future. You will be able to save for all your financial goals given enough time. For the unexpected goals, you have an emergency fund. You will also avail of services that will prepare you for possible emergencies like accidents and hospitalization.

- You will be able to prevent bad financial practices that may destroy your future

One of the key principles of budgeting is constant awareness of where your money is going. In the steps to creating your budgeting system, you will be instructed to take note of all your expenses. By keeping track of all your expenses, you will be able to examine your past expenses. You will be able to identify categories of expenses that hurt your financial life the most. When you have identified them, you will be able to prevent these bad spending activities from becoming habits.

- It will keep your family happy and contented

A family that budgets is generally happier and more contented with life. An effective budgeter is always ahead in paying his bills. He does not react towards expenses. He tries to anticipate them and implement strategies to deal with them even when the deadline is still far. If you deal with expenses this way, life will be a lot less stressful.

- You will be able to teach your children how to of budget, save and reach their financial goals

If you practice budgeting consistently, you will be able to teach your children the financial principles that you follow by being a good example to them. You will be able to show them the importance of delayed gratification.

If you want them to learn how to budget properly, you should teach them the process of budgeting. You should also make them aware of the common bad spending practices that may prevent them from implementing their budget plan properly. You should make them focus on the family's goals. You should also show consistency when practicing your budgeting plan, especially when spending in front of your children. If your children see that budgeting can be done successfully, they will be more confident with their money management skills when they become adults.

Discovering Your Motivational Sources

You need to be the one to discover what motivates you to budget and save money. You must already have a reason for buying this book. You need to reawaken that reason right now by answering this question:

Why do you want to budget your money?

If that does not help, you can narrow it down by picking one of these more specific questions:

Who motivates you to budget and save?

What do you want to buy if you are successful in budgeting and saving?

By reflecting on these questions, you will be able to find your reason for budgeting. You should write down your reason by creating a dream statement. This is a sentence or a paragraph that will remind you of your reason for budgeting.

Some people budget to save for an expensive purchase. Others prefer to pay big for experiences like traveling to unique places around the world. For some, their source of motivation is closer to home. They want to save to provide their children with a good college education.

When you write your dream state, you need to make it personal by using the right words. You need to use specific words. Instead of saying:

I want to save for my son's college education.

You should say:

I am saving for Michael's college education at MIT.

This statement is a message from your younger self to your older self. By stating the child's name, the message becomes more personal every time you read it. We also changed the tense used in the statement. From future tense, we changed it to the present tense. This signifies that you are already doing the action. You start budgeting the moment you decide on your goal and write it down. You never stop budgeting until your reach your goals.

You should then write your dream statement on multiple pieces of paper. You should tape a statement to all your credit cards. You should also put a copy of this in your wallet. It should be visible when you open your wallet. This will remind you of what you are saving for, every time you open your wallet. In most instances, you will make the better financial judgment when you see these reminders. This technique will only fail if you ignore your dream statements when you see them. You need to make it a habit to read your statement out loud when you see it.

Make self-talk a habit

Most people buy on impulse. They do not put a lot of thought when making purchases. If you tend to do the same, you should develop a habit of stopping and thinking before making a purchase.

You do not have to make a complicated argument out of every purchase. All you have to do is to ask yourself this question before each purchase:

Am I making a financially wise decision?

You should answer this question by talking to yourself out loud. We tend to make wiser decisions when we hear our reasoning behind our actions. It is also easier to lie to ourselves if we only use our mind to justify a purchase. We tend to become ashamed of the lies we tell when we hear ourselves say it.

CHAPTER 4: HOW TO GET OVER COMPULSIVE SPENDING HABITS

What is Compulsive Spending?

Have you ever watched the movie Confessions of a Shopaholic? It is a sweet, better-than-it-looks rom-com about a young journalist who is addicted to shopping. She is trapped in the maze of credit cards, collecting a debt of more than $16,000. She lives in a constant terror of debt collectors, she doesn't pay her rent for a few months, but she still can't stop shopping.

In the movie, it is not mentioned, but she has a compulsive buying disorder (CBD), or oniomania. In practice, this means that a person has obsessive shopping habits that bring adverse consequences for them.

Compulsive buying disorder can be triggered by perfectionism, the desire of perceived acceptance by others, the need for control, or general impulsiveness. However, it can also be a manifestation of identity searching, social position-gaining hopes, or anxiety, low self-confidence or depression. These reasons do not apply to all cases. Not everybody who experiences CBD suffers from depression.

For those who are wealthy, CBD might just seem like an everyday pastime. In many cases it is. For those who have a tight budget, this condition can ruin their lives. Those who need budgeting the most should consider reading more about CBD.

The recent popularity gain of online shopping doesn't help people with CBD but rather fuels them. They can get lost for hours or days in an online shopping rabbit hole, bringing severe consequences to their work or personal life. Sometimes people with CBD use online shopping as an escape from reality.

The difference between CBD and regular shopping is the compulsive, overwhelming desire to buy and spend against the better judgment or known negative consequences. Non-addicted buyers buy for the sake of real need and utility, while compulsive buyers buy for mood-improvement and balancing emotions.

Just like other addictions, buying disorder roots in dissatisfied emotional needs. Since we know by now that ads primarily trigger emotions, it's not hard to imagine how it affects a person who craves satisfying that need. It feels like drugs – it gives a bit of relief when the purchase satisfies the need, but soon the positive effects fade. A new, bigger dose of satisfaction will be needed.

People suffering from CBD think just as intensely and as often about shopping as an alcoholic about the next drink.

Is Compulsive Buying a Mental Health Issue?

We live in a culture where money talks. Better said, objects that you buy with money talk. Everything encourages consumerism and sells the belief that what you drive, wear, or Facebook on actually defines you. Items are the key to happiness and success.

Many people expect social acceptance, self-image, self-worth and self-esteem improvement from their purchases. Buying things for immediate personal gratification is the new black. Overspending our budget, however, can easily get out of control since it is so easy to get credit cards today. People with CBD, however, have a more complex problem than "retail therapy."

As I said before, compulsive buying serves the temporary enhancement of emotional need satisfaction. This emotion-regulation strategy swings between apprehension or anxiety to a temporary feeling of frenzy and positive excitement during the research and purchase of something. This compulsive, vicious buying cycle usually culminates in guilt or remorse. When the realization of how much money one spent on usually useless items overshadows the positive clouds, bitter regret falls on them. The regret soon transforms into anxiety. And guess where they end up "treating" their anxiety? Yes, a shop. The circle starts over again.

The answer to the question "Is compulsive buying a mental health issue?" is no. Compulsive spending behavior itself is not a diagnosable mental health condition. It's more a symptom of other psychological issues, like the insufficient sense of self-worth or addiction. According to some researchers, CBD is a form of obsessive-compulsive disorder. Others consider it something akin to an impulse control problem where the person seeks short-term gratification while ignoring long-term consequences.

Compulsive spending in most cases results in compulsive hoarding. People who give such great value to inanimate objects tend to feel cumulated satisfaction with the more they have. Hoarding items can also give a false sense of security – I'm closely affected by this problem. This leads, however, to another issue. On the one hand, the more things hoarders own, the more secure they feel. On the other, the more they have, the more terrified they become of losing it all.

How to Overcome Compulsive Buying

The easiest and quickest way to overcome compulsive buying is to raise better emotional awareness. The best way is to work with a licensed therapist. An objective, unbiased third party, can help you stay on track better than your friends and family. Also, a professional can help you with healthy emotion regulation strategies to understand where your compulsive buying tendencies come from and overcome the urge of mindless buying in the future. The therapist can help you identify the causes and negative consequences of your actions, and help you figure out replacement actions for the compulsive behavior.

It is important to examine the positive and negative sides of the compulsive buying behavior to find an appropriate alternative lifestyle that satisfies needs while being less self-destructive.

There are no specific therapies designed solely to overcome compulsive shopping habits, but there are many forms of therapy that can help people address this issue. Two therapies produce outstanding positive results: cognitive behavioral therapy, and therapies using different mindfulness techniques. The former proves to be the best when used in groups. Two psychologists, Michel Lejoyeux and Aviv Weinstein, researched the efficacy of cognitive behavioral therapy in case of CBD. They highlighted that a proper psychiatric evaluation should precede the therapy to find the most appropriate recovery program for the patient. If the patient receives the most appropriate therapy, it will decrease their compulsive buying tendencies after only ten weeks of participation. The latter, the mindfulness technique, therapies resulted in impulse improvement, better emotion management, and acceptance.

People with compulsive buying tendencies might want to add financial counseling along with their psychotherapy. Anything can be useful, from self-help books to online finance and budgeting courses, to group counseling meetings. Raising financial awareness and budgeting improvement techniques can help a lot with facing the financial reality of a person with CBD.

If you feel that you suffer from a milder or more severe, version of CBD you might want to consult a counselor about it. From a budgeting point of view, it is critical to keep your shopping impulses under control. Otherwise, even if you manage to budget and save in the short term, you won't be able to keep it in the long-term.

CHAPTER 5: TACKLING CREDIT CARD DEBT

The Most Important Rule

When it comes to paying bills (any bill – not just your credit card bills), it is important to remember this: always pay on time. When you don't pay your bills on time, many things can happen:

1. You get charged a late fee. The good news is (yes, there is good news), depending on your history with this particular company, you could call them up ahead of time and tell them that you won't be able to make a payment on time. They might wave the late fee for you. Of course, this won't happen if you're regularly late.

2. Your interest rate will go up. Did you know that some companies will increase your rate up to 15% after just one late payment? While you've got them on the phone, make sure to ask them about your interest rate and if it will increase because of this. Don't worry about trying to negotiate with them either. Sure, you can't slip him a twenty when you shake hands (I could never perfect that move), but a little ethical negotiation isn't wrong. Ethical negotiation = don't auction off your first born.

3. It's a ding on your credit report (when your payment is more than a month late). It's incredibly important for you to pay your late amount (and fees) as soon as you can. The longer you wait, the more chance that the company will report your late payment.

4. Your credit score drops. Did you know that payment history makes up over a third of your credit score? That's why late payments have such a big effect on your overall score. Remember that emergency phone call that you made to try and avoid that late fee? You can also ask them if this will impact your credit score. A lot of companies won't report a

late payment right away (grace periods are awesome and convenient) but don't take their generosity for granted.

Another Important Rule

Okay, I take that back. Paying on time is the most important but at a close second is: Pull your free credit report every year to keep a close eye on your credit score. There are a ton of places that offer free versions of your credit score.

Your Credit Card Debt

One of the big ways for you to save money is to tackle your credit card debt. Once you pay off all of those credit cards, you'll have more money to save or to spend on other necessities after all.

Snowball Method

The snowball method can be traced back to the famous Dave Ramsey, the financial guru. This method is based on the theory that you should start paying off the smallest balance first. Once you pay that off, you move on to the next one.

Use the money that you would have otherwise been using to pay off the smallest account on top of this regular payment. After that's paid off, do the same with the next one. Use the money that you would have otherwise used on the first two cards to add on to your regular payment.

Not only that, but the snowball method also helps build your confidence as you pay off your smaller debts. Because you can see progress faster, you feel better about saving money and paying off your debts. It feels good to see that progress.

Avalanche Method

This method requires that you list off your credit card (or other) debts by interest rate. Place the largest interest rate first and descend from that. Pay off the debt with the highest interest rate first. This makes it so you will pay off your debt faster and you spend less money on just plain interest.

This plan makes a lot of sense logically, but you have to have some strong will-power to stick to your plan.

Your Credit Score Is Important.

There are many different ways to mess up your credit score. Here are three big ways for you to mess up your credit without even trying:

1. Use up Your Available Credit.

Yep, there are other ways to destroy your credit card too – and this is one of them. Don't take their $15,000 credit limit as a challenge. Your credit utilization ratio (how much credit you're actually using) is extremely influential in figuring out what your credit score is.

So if you have $15,000 of available credit and you use up $14,999, you could be doing your credit card and your credit score harm. The best ratios are 10% or lower, but on average, you should aim for about 30%.

2. Maxing Out More Than One Card

Not only is this a great way to destroy a credit card, but it'll also do a number on your credit score. This ruins your credit score because it messes with your credit utilization ratio – like when you use up your available credit by maxing out a card. Just imagine what will happen if you max out more than one of your cards.

3. Closing Your Highest Limit Card First

Remember credit utilization ratio I talked about at number one? Consider this: you've got a card with a $20,000 limit and one with a $2,000 limit. Altogether, you've got $22,000 of available credit. Supposing you've got a 3,000 dollar balance on the card with the highest limit, and $1,000 on the smaller card - that still leaves you with $17,000 of credit and a credit utilization ratio of about 22%.

Okay, let's say that you pay off and close out the card with the highest limit. That knocks your available credit to only $2,000. Your ratio then skyrockets to 50% and your credit score won't like that number.

Things You Should Know About Credit Cards

Having been in the situation where I didn't know what I was doing when I first acquired my first credit card, I found that knowledge is one of the best things you can arm yourself with.

1. Having a credit card doesn't mean that you have to use it or be in debt.

It isn't black and white. You don't have to keep it locked up or be forever in debt. There are other ways of using credit cards. It is possible for you to use your credit card regularly and stay out of debt by charging only what you can afford to pay when the bill arrives each month. Of course, to do this, you have to make sure that you keep a close eye on how much you are spending.

2. You can easily create a repayment plan by yourself or with the aid of creditors (though it would be nice not to have to get them involved).

Unlike popular belief, companies do want you to pay them back. They don't want you forever in debt. Creditors and collection companies will work with you to develop a repayment plan. You can even work with a credit counselor if you need some advice on coming up with a plan that gets you out of the red but still allows for you to live a fun and healthy life.

3. You can't go to jail for nonpayment, but they can take a lot from you.

If you have credit card debt and you don't pay it off, you won't go to prison. However, the companies can sue you and garnish your wages or assets as the judge sees fit.

4. If you don't pay on time, there are a bunch of hidden fees to watch out for.

Let's say that you close a credit card account without actually looking at the final statement. That little balance can grow into a gigantic monster because of late fees, interest, and default APR. Not only that, there is a specific residual interest that is generated after the bill is issued and before your payment is received. If you can, always pay your balance in full, all the time. Don't stop making payments after you close the account.

5. Don't go applying for every credit card out there.

Having credit available all the time is good for your credit score so the theory stands that if you can get a credit card, you should apply for it, right? Wrong. Every time you apply for a credit card, and you get rejected, it's a ding on your credit score.

6. Double your sign up bonus.

Sign up bonuses can be great and they don't always come around so have your spouse or partner apply for the same card to double up on those bonuses. Just make sure that you keep a close eye on how much you spend. Just because those bonuses are there, doesn't mean that they will be there forever and that you can't overspend.

7. Gift cards can be used in creative ways too.

If you need to reach a minimum spending threshold to get a sign-up bonus, use your credit card to purchase gift cards for stores that you visit often. You can even use your credit card to buy cash cards. Just make sure that you buy the cards before the deadline. Then you can use the gift cards later. Here's another trick. If you get bonus points on your card for shopping at certain places, like your local grocery store, buy your gift cards there to get the points, get the sign-up bonus, and have the gift cards to use later.

CHAPTER 6: CREATING YOUR BUDGETING SYSTEM

When budgeting, you are balancing between your essential needs, your wants and your financial goals. Here are the steps on how you can achieve this balance:

Step 1: Identify your financial priorities

The first step requires you to list all the things that you want in your life that requires a financial commitment. To do this, you need to anticipate future financial needs.

Identifying future financial needs

Before you can start a budget plan, you need to think of your life goals. This is not a very difficult task for most people. We all know what we want to buy if we had some extra money. Some of us want to travel around the world for example, while others just want to buy items that bring them comfort in their own homes.

When we talk about goals in this chapter, however, we are not talking about consumer products or entertaining services. We are talking about important life milestones that require money. Buying a house, for instance, is a worthwhile goal. Everybody wants his or her own home. The urgency becomes even greater when you are planning to have a family. You need a home where your family can grow.

A person with no insight will not think of this problem until it is urgent. A wiser person would anticipate this future need and prepare for it financially when he still has a lot of time. You need to think about your future financial needs right after this paragraph. You need to list them all down and put them in order according to their importance.

Adding your passion in the list

Life would be dull if we only worked for what we need. The mind needs a little excitement now and then. If we think life is exciting, we are more motivated to work.

This is where your passions come in. Aside from your needs, you also need to provide funds for your passions. If you love traveling, you can still do it even if you are following a budget, as long as it is planned and your income justifies such trips.

You should take this time to think of the few luxuries that you will allow yourself and your loved ones to enjoy. You need to have the discipline not to overdo these luxuries. You should only do them to re-motivate yourself and the other members of your family to continue saving.

Step 2: Set the right amount of money for your needs and wants

Now that you know what you need to save for, you need to make a monthly expenses list. When making your list, you need to divide all your expenses into categories. Here are some of the common expense categories:

- Food
- Utility bills
- Transportation expenses
- Toiletries, laundry and other home maintenance expenses

These are the expenses common to all adults. Some people, however, have other expense categories in their lives. Here are some examples:

- Kids' needs
- Sports and fitness
- Pets

In some months, you will also need to spend money on additional important things. If you have a new job, for example, you may need new clothes that will make you fit in. If this is the case, you may need to include a clothes budget for that month. For the holidays, you will also need to include gifts and holiday food categories. By including these seasonal expenses, you will be prepared financially for all of them.

You should also make special categories for specific types of expenses that you wish to keep track of. If you are guilty of spending too much on eating out, for example, you may need to cut back on this category. However, we usually include this category with food expenses. To keep track of your total dining-out expenses, you need to make a special category for it and separate it from the food category.

After listing all your expense categories, you need to know how much money each category needs every month. The amount that you should set aside for food, for example, depends on the number of people in your family. You need to set fixed amounts for these categories.

You should also anticipate the amount that you need to spend on categories that do not have a fixed price. Your electricity bill, for example, varies every month. You need to prepare for the ups and downs of these types of expenses.

Employing a budgeting rule

Aside from the strategies discussed above, you can also apply a budgeting rule to make sure that you do not overspend every month. Here are some of them:

80-10-10 Rule

The 80-10-10 rule is the easiest one to follow. This rule generally means that you spend 80% of your net income on your needs and wants. 10% of your income should go to charity while the last 10% should go to your savings. The rule allows you to share your income with your community while still saving for your long-term goals.

60-10-30 Rule

This rule is stricter than the one above. You can use it if you can live comfortably with 60% of your net income. 10% still goes to charity, and the 30% goes to your savings. By saving a bigger part of your income, you will be able to reach your financial goals faster.

50% Rule

You should use this rule when you have debts to pay or when there is an urgent short-term goal that you need to reach. In this budgeting rule, you try to make all your needs and wants fit with only 50% of your net income. The other 50% is allocated to your savings. If your needs and wants still go beyond your 50% of your income, you need to cut back on some less important expense categories.

Step 3: Adjust your lifestyle and goals according to your income level

At this point, you already know about the things that you need to spend on right now and the future financial commitments that you need to save for. By now, you should already know if your monthly income would allow you to fund your lifestyle and save for your future financial goals.

If you are one of the lucky ones, there may be some excess money left after all your expenses and savings. For most people, however, the income they bring in will not be enough to fund their current lifestyle and save for big goals at the same time. If you have the same experience, you should consider readjusting some areas of your life.

You should first check some of the categories that you listed above and the corresponding amount allocated for these funds. You should identify areas where you can cut back so that you will have more money for savings.

Increase your income

If your income is low, no amount of cutbacks will allow you to save. If you still cannot save after serious cutbacks in all your spending categories, you should find opportunities that will increase your income. If your goals require a large amount of money and you only have a short period to save for it, you also need to take this approach.

Step 4: Allocate your money as soon as you receive it

When your income arrives, the first thing that you need to do is to distribute them properly. The first allocation should go to your savings. By setting money aside as soon as you receive them, you will not be tempted to spend too much on groceries or shopping.

The next categories that you need to allocate for are your basic needs, important utility bills, and other important payments. You should not neglect these areas because it is very inconvenient if you miss these payments.

The next area that you need to allocate for is your basic needs. You need to set money aside for food and groceries.

The amount left should be distributed to all the other important expenses that you have listed. If there is still some left after allocating your money, you may spend some part of it for your entertainment or your passions. You may also allocate the money for next month's expenses.

If you receive extra amounts, you have a choice to add it to your savings or to spend it for things and experiences that bring short-term happiness. We recommend that you save it for your goals. The more money you save, the faster you will reach your financial goals.

Step 5: Track your money

As mentioned in the previous chapters, you need to be aware of where your money is going. Money flows in and out of your budget fund. You should make sure that more money goes in than out. To be able to know where your money is going, you need to take note of where every penny is going.

By tracking your money, you will be able to make sure that you are following your planned budget. If you notice that you are spending too fast in the food category, for example, you could take measures that will allow you to keep your food expenses low.

To be able to track your money easily, you need a tool that you are familiar with. Here are some of the common tools used by expert budgeters:

1. Notebook and ledger

The easiest tool to use is a notebook that will serve as a logbook where you place all of your expenses for the day. It needs to be small enough that you can carry around. Before the day ends, you should transfer your records to a bigger ledger. You can consult your ledger to analyze your spending habits.

2. Smartphone app

If you are a smartphone user, there are free apps that will allow you to replace the notebook system. Every time you spend, you can just bring out your smartphone and list your expenses. You need to make this activity a habit every time you spend. This is a better option than a notebook because we bring our phone everywhere we go. Unlike the notebook, the app does not become full easily. If it becomes full, you only need to uninstall the app and reinstall it to wipe records away.

There are premium apps available that provide these types of services, but if you do not have the budget, there are also free apps that offer limited features. For most people, the features of the free apps are enough to keep a daily, weekly and monthly record of their expenses.

3. Spreadsheet

Instead of a ledger, you should use a spreadsheet file to store all your expense data. If you are familiar with using this type of tool, you will be able to make calculations faster and make fast interpretations of data presented.

You can use Numbers for Mac or Microsoft Excel if you have these programs on your computer. If not, you can also use open source options available for download online. The open source options' features are enough for this purpose.

Tips on tracking your expenses:

- Keep track of even the smallest expenses

People who are new to tracking their money tend to neglect the small expenses. You should keep in mind that all the small expenses add up. Over the course of 6 months or a year, these small expenses will add up to a big amount.

- Keep your tracking descriptions accurate

When checking your expenses in, you need to provide all your notes with accurate descriptions. If you make vague descriptions, you may not remember where the payment was made, and you may not be able to categorize the expenses properly.

- Keep receipts or notes when you don't have your tracking tools

There are times when your tracking tools are not available. Your phone may be dead, or your notebook may be full. That is why you should always ask for a receipt for all your purchases. If a receipt is not available, you should ask for a piece of paper from the payee so that you can make a note of all your expenses. You should place these notes in your wallet and go back to them at the end of the day.

- Check your expenses record every 12 hours

In the beginning, it will be difficult for you to take note of all of your expenses. You may miss some expenses when you are in a hurry. To prevent lapses in recording your expenses, you should set your alarm for 12 hours. When the alarm goes off, you should set aside whatever you are doing and check if your spending records are complete. You will know if you missed taking note of some expenses if there is a discrepancy between your records and the cash left in your wallet.

CONCLUSION

Thank you again for downloading this book!

I hope this book was able to help you to organize and control your finances more easily.

Finally, if you enjoyed this book, then I'd like to ask you for a favor, would you be kind enough to leave a review for this book on Amazon? It'd be greatly appreciated!

Thank you and good luck!

www.ingramcontent.com/pod-product-compliance
Lightning Source LLC
Chambersburg PA
CBHW030059230526
45471CB00003B/1169